Published by
Meadow Geese Press, Incorporated
Box 345, Marshfield Hills, Massachusetts, 02051

Text © 2000 Estate of Beverley T. Thomas
Illustrations © 2000 Karen A. Jerome
Poem written by Nancy Byrd Turner (1880-1971)

Design and Electronic Composition by James Aromaa Design
The illustrations are done in watercolors

First Edition, First Printing
Printed in China

ISBN: 0-9665564-1-0

Library of Congress Catalog Card Number: 00-101140

when it rained cats and dogs

Nancy Byrd Turner

Illustrated by Karen A. Jerome

Dedicated to the memory of
Beverley T. Thomas and
William H. B. Thomas

S.A.

To Theresa "Bong" Andrews

K.A.J.

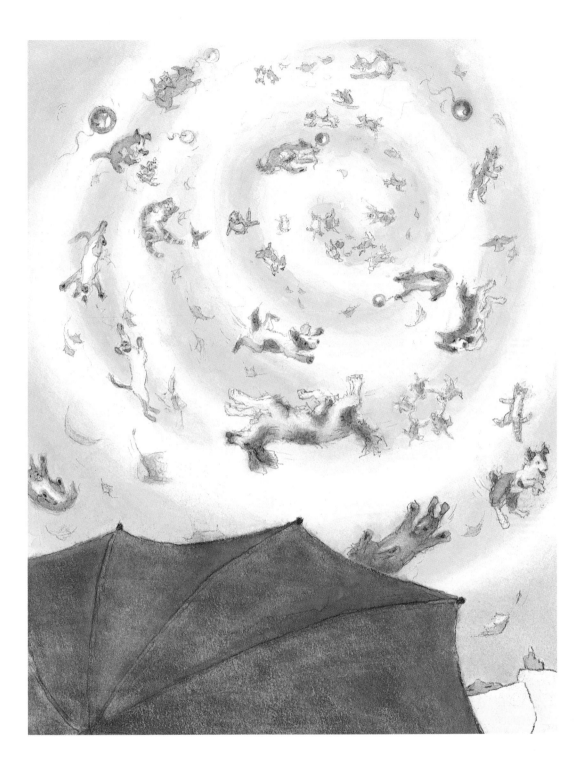

Did you ever hear of the wonderful day
when it rained in the most remarkable way?

There weren't any mists,
There weren't any fogs,
it just rained nothing
but cats and dogs.

Of every color
and every size,
cats and dogs
rained out
of the skies.

Slim ones,
pudgy ones,
large and small,
and not a
single one
hurt at all.

Half a dozen with flips and flops

slithered over umbrella tops.

Children were running
here and there,
scooping them up
from everywhere.

Poodles
from puddles

and
charming
Chows,

Cocker Spaniels from bushes and boughs.

A Collie, a Shepherd, a Boston Bull,

were rained down into a swimming pool.

A chubby kitten as yellow as butter,

bobbed up cheerfully

out of a gutter.

And still the cats and dogs came tumbling down,

raining, raining, on country and town.

Excellent pups
and mannerly kits,
ready for catnip
or bones or bits.

Over and over for one whole hour

odd things happened in that odd shower.

Till there wasn't a single home without
one of the creatures, for miles about.

And people still tell
in the joyfullest way
of the wonderful shower
that fell on that day.

There weren't any mists, there weren't any fogs...

it just rained nothing but

cats and dogs.